Dear Mother,

I thot this was so cute and hope you well too.

Love,
Bill, Jane
Jack + Becky

ONCE

UPON A

CHRISTMAS

TIME

OTHER BOOKS

BY THYRA FERRÉ BJORN

PAPA'S WIFE

PAPA'S DAUGHTER

MAMA'S WAY

A TRILOGY, containing

PAPA'S WIFE, PAPA'S DAUGHTER,

and MAMA'S WAY

DEAR PAPA

ONCE

UPON A

CHRISTMAS

TIME

by

THYRA FERRÉ BJORN

HOLT, RINEHART AND
WINSTON
NEW YORK   CHICAGO
SAN FRANCISCO

Published simultaneously in Canada by
Holt, Rinehart and Winston of Canada,
Limited.

Library of Congress
Catalog Card Number: 64-21934

Published, November, 1964
Second Printing, November, 1964
Third Printing, April, 1965
Fourth Printing, November, 1965

Designer: Ernst Reichl

80973-0614

Printed in the U.S.A.

To my four brothers

George

Nels

Folke

Gustave

Who shared with their four sisters

the many wonderful

Once Upon a Christmas Times

in our beloved parsonage,

this book is fondly dedicated

To My Readers:

This book is made up of informal recollections, of memories locked until now within my own heart. It is a glimpse into years gone by and the beauty those years contained. I have not done any research on the matters about which I have written, for all are things I have been told firsthand or have experienced myself. My aim was to have the reminiscences flow from my heart and mind as spontaneously as one offers a warm handshake or a fleeting smile.

In today's busy world we don't take time to fill our souls with beauty. I pray that each one who reads these pages will pause long enough to recapture Yules long gone and perhaps to find back there in time the key to happiness and contentment in this restless age.

Let us make this Christmas a returning home, a sharing of happiness with the family and all those around us.

Longmeadow, Massachusetts

ONCE

UPON A

CHRISTMAS

TIME

ONE

IT BELONGS to all of us, this mood of once-upon-a-time, and at no period of the year do we feel it more than at Christmas. There is no season of more tender memories, of sweeter, gentler thoughts than that of which we remind one another annually, saying, "Do you remember . . . ?" Our childhood yuletides glow with a light brighter than all the brilliant space-age colors, a glow that will never dim as ages go by.

My own once-upon-a-time goes back many years to my native Sweden. What a perfect setting for a story! A land where snow lay deep and white and a million stars shone down on the silence of the night of nights. As a child with a vivid imagination, I could almost see those angels hovering over the stable in Bethlehem, singing their glory to God. And if I listened with my magic ear, I could hear the footsteps of shepherds coming closer and closer to the place where the star shone most brightly. It would have been hard for me to understand that snow was not part of that first Christmas, because how could it possibly be Christmas without that glistening white blanket?

In my homeland the holiday did not come on the twenty-fifth of the month. It crept its magic way through much of December. Steeped as Sweden is in ancient tradition and folklore, everything seemed to have a special meaning. There are many customs that belong to December alone and that have been repeated over and over for hundreds of years. Some of them, of course, were rooted in superstition that has now been lost in the shuffle of time. I am sure that in modern Sweden there is not a person left who believes that trolls and goblins and gnomes really exist. They do not take seriously the idea that one who sets foot outside his home on Christmas Eve can be bewitched. Nor do they believe in the weird tales that their loved ones have a chance to come back to earth and to their homes each Christmas Eve. They think it foolishness that people in olden times gave up their own beds and left food on the table for the returning dead, and they scoff at the notion that ghosts met in the old church at precisely twelve midnight to conduct their own Christmas services. They shrug off as just another old tale that one bold farmer who decided to peek into the church on a Christmas Eve really saw them all sitting there; and that, hurrying home, he was taken ill and did not live very long thereafter.

Nevertheless, these tales had a strange charm for us as children; we sat fascinated by the stories told to us by our grandmothers, knowing that they had been passed down from generation to generation. And even as we outgrew many of the superstitions, it was still hard to realize that our beloved *Tomte* was a myth and that he did not really eat the big bowlful of rice-porridge that we set on the doorstep for him each Christmas Eve.

The Swedish *Tomte*, although very similar to the American Santa Claus, was much more than a myth and a tradition. He was a cross between an Irish leprechaun and Holland's St. Nicholaus, and more than just a Christmas symbol because the *Tomte* lived on Swedish farms throughout the whole year. Each farm had its own *Tomte*, and if you treated him well, he brought good luck to the household. But if you neglected his welfare, terrible things could happen to the farm animals and everything could go wrong. He is hundreds of years old, but it is only in recent centuries that he has been bringing gifts at Christmas time, traveling around the world, doing good for good children.

It was easy enough to assign him that role, however, for he was both loved and feared; and on Christmas Eve that big bowl of rice left for him on the doorstep was a token of love and appreciation from the household for his faithful watch over the farm. The *Tomte* was so much a part of life that none of us, as children, ever stopped to figure out that he could not possibly be real. It was a pleasure to be blind to the things we did not want to change. But in this modern age, the *Tomte* has been reduced to a mere Christmas elf who watches to see if children are good or bad and rewards them with gifts accordingly.

He will be one of the last of the old Swedish folk-tales to be discarded; for if he were, Christmas would lose its glamour for children and would become just another holy day when gifts are exchanged. But, looking back, I am glad that as a child I believed that the *Tomte* existed and that I almost saw him many times when my imagination was working at its best. It filled me with joy that I was sometimes given the honor of placing the bowl of rice on the doorstep. The glow of that experience always warms my heart as I go back into the Christmas yesteryears.

Sweden is an old country, which had its beginning about five hundred years before the first Christmas. It had been just a little plot of land, rising up out of the great waters, but as the waters receded and the land grew in size, people came there to live and claimed it as their country. There were hundreds of dark years when the people worshiped heathen gods, and strange and mysterious are the tales of Tor, Oden, and Freja and numberless other gods. Many of the traditions and superstitions from the heathen world lingered on when Sweden became a Christian country. People seeking for the light did not discard immediately or completely their belief in evil spirits and strange beings. But as the years passed by, more and more of the old was swallowed up by the new and young and beautiful, and many ugly tales were discarded like useless old tools. But they did not get rid of them all, and perhaps they never will as long as Sweden is Sweden and Christmas comes during the darkest time of the year.

Yes, during the long, dark, cold winter nights the old ones told the children tales never written down, but repeated to generation after generation. Perhaps a little was added here and there to suit each narrator's fancy or to make a child's eyes grow bigger and rounder as he listened. And some details were probably omitted now and then for lack of memory. Perhaps that is why some stories have several versions and different meanings for different individuals.

The old lady who often took care of us children in the parsonage when Mama and Papa had to attend meetings and conferences was an expert storyteller. How I loved to snuggle up to her and listen to her soft voice! I often hoped that she would talk forever and that bedtime would never come.

It was this old lady, with a network of hundreds of wrinkles in her dear old face, who first told me about Saint Lucia. I have since learned that the legends about Lucia are many, but I shall always like best the story I heard first, and in my heart I liked to believe that it is the real one. When time goes back hundreds of years, it is very far for a little girl to conceive of completely.

Christmas to me began on the thirteenth of December when all of Sweden celebrated the Festival of Lights. On that morning the oldest daughter in the household got up long before daybreak to prepare coffee to serve to the rest of the family in bed. It was only to the oldest girl that this honored tradition belonged. To fathom its beauty, one must see and experience it. We must first bear in mind the thick darkness of the time of year and the cold that gripped my little snow country. What fun to make ready and finally to light the seven tall tapers of the candle-crown and place it on one's hair. Then to pick up the coffee tray on which have been placed the best round, embroidered white cloth, coffee cups for all the members of the family, the fat "Lucia cats" buns made especially for this morning, and finally the bright copper coffee pot filled with steaming coffee. It was a long slow walk from room to room, but what a picture the Lucia bride made; her face so sweet and young, her golden hair falling softly over her shoulders, her eyes shining as brightly as the candles in her crown. It was a vision almost unearthly in its beauty.

The song she sang as she walked from bed to bed, waking each person to serve him coffee, wove a spell with tune and words:

> Night walks with heavy tread
> In cottage and garden.
> Shadows hover over the land
> Deserted by the sun.
> And in our dark house
> Santa Lucia Walks.
> > Santa Lucia,
> > Santa Lucia.

The song had many verses and in Swedish it was beautiful. It proclaimed that soon the darkness would flee and the sun would step out of the rosy sky and all would be well. And we who belonged to Sweden echoed her song in our hearts. The tradition is a very, very old one, but its glow has never faded. The candles shine just as brightly year after year, and the story of

Saint Lucia is as pure and fresh as the long white flowing gown the Lucia bride wears on that special morning.

And my heart still beats with excitement and wonder as in memory I hear again the voice of the old storyteller, relating to me for the very first time the Lucia legend.

The first Lucia was not a Swedish girl; she was born in Sicily where certain events took place in the year 304. I wondered as I listened how the world had looked way back then. It must have been very different. But one thing was the same and that was love. I understood that; and love was much a part of the story of Lucia with whose festival in December the Christmas season begins.

Lucia, was very, very beautiful, and much of her beauty was in her eyes which reflected a soul sweet and pure. To look into them was like seeing a bit of God's beautiful heaven. Eternal things seemed to fill her mind, and she lived to do good deeds, especially for those in need.

As the custom was in those days, her father gave her in marriage to a young man of the village. Just at that time, Lucia's mother was taken very ill; and Lucia, who adored her, sat by her side as death seemed about to claim her. Lucia prayed for her mother's recovery, pleading with God, and promising that if He restored her mother's health, she would give all her worldly possessions to the oppressed Christians.

Her prayers were answered; and when her mother's health was restored, Lucia knew it was a miracle and that she must keep her promise to God. So she gave all that her father had given her as a dowry, every bit of it, to the poor; and her husband received nothing in worldly goods when he took his lovely young bride.

He, not understanding her deed, became very, very angry; he accused Lucia of witchcraft, for he believed that no one in her right mind could have done what she did. Lucia was tried and burned at the stake.

But, the legend says, as her limp body crumpled under the cruel fire, the whole village was illuminated by a brilliant light; and the heartless, ignorant people became frightened because they suddenly understood that the girl was a saint, not a witch, and that it was goodness which had prompted her to give her wealth to the needy.

Thereafter she was seen again and again in many different places where people needed help. And once she appeared in the province of Värmland to feed the people dying of starvation, thus endearing herself to the Swedish people. Eventually she was canonized by the Church of Rome, and so lives on in the world today.

The Lucia bride is still a symbol, in Sweden, a symbol of hope and peace and light in the darkest season of the year. The celebration in her memory is a festive occasion when hundreds of Swedish girls compete for the honor of being selected as the year's outstanding Lucia bride.

The tradition has spilled over to the Swedish-American churches and organizations and, on the thirteenth of each December, the most beautiful girl is chosen by the people to march down the aisle with the lighted candle-crown on her lovely head, in a special service symbolizing new light and joy for our world.

TWO

FOLLOWING the thirteenth of December, with the warm glow of the beautiful saint still in our thoughts, the great preparations began for the fast-approaching holidays. One of the first of these was the making of hundreds and hundreds of cookies. These were baked early in the month, placed in tightly covered tins, and stored in the cold earth cellar, not to be opened until the afternoon of the day before Christmas when, according to an old tradition, folks were allowed to taste them for the first time.

So imbedded was this in our minds that we children never even asked for a cookie, no matter how good they looked to us. I smile to myself now as I wander back in time. What a perfect tradition that was! I wonder if it wasn't some old Granny who came up with it in the beginning to keep her cookies safe from both children and adults. It was handy to have as a threat the dark omen that terrible things would happen to the individual or to the household if the tradition were broken.

Very, very early on the baking morning, housewives would leave their warm beds, tiptoing softly so as not to awaken the rest of the household. Bracing themselves, they would go down into the ice-cold kitchen where thick frost flowers had formed on the window-panes, and they would scrape off a little and look out into the dense darkness, hoping that there would be a tiny sliver of a new moon in the sky, because nothing else could give better luck to the baking procedure. The white vapor from their own breath was visible before the fire was lit in the blackwood stove that would soon give out plenty of heat. How quickly the fire began to burn since all the preparations had been made the night before. There was dry bark in a pile beside the logs, and perhaps, if the household were lucky, there were a few *tyre* sticks. This wood had in it a certain substance that made the fire flare up quickly and ignite the small white logs. It was a matter of careful planning, and every Swedish housewife took pride in being efficient. Carefully trained by her mother in all household tasks, each woman strove to be the best and most clever of all.

Soon the kitchen began to take on a feeling of warmth and hominess as the copper coffeepot began to bubble while the oven was heating, and the many different doughs were being mixed.

Each cookie was a unique creation, from an unwritten recipe which was followed step by step. I never remember Mama having anything written down on paper. It was all committed to memory. She took just so much of this and so much of that; there was just so much time for mixing, so many strokes with the wire wisk. It was done the same way year after year, and nothing was ever changed or forgotten.

As the glowing fire warmed the big kitchen, a bit of heathendom lurked in the dark corners. How long it had existed, no one seemed to know. Few housewives ever reflected on the reason they baked so early in the morning. It had always been that way; their mothers before them and their grandmothers and great grandmothers had all arisen at this unearthly hour to begin the Christmas-cookie baking.

But the old story lady could tell us that it had started way back in the dark ages. The baking of fancy things at this darkest time of the year began when the cookies were made to celebrate the Festival of the Lights which was held annually to drive away the spirits of darkness and to appease the gods who held the powers of good and evil for the people and the land. It was the gods who had proclaimed and made it an established rule that no sunlight should shine on this dough. If it did, disaster would fall on the household and its people. I have a feeling that this tradition has been almost completely done away with in modern Sweden, but tales are still told of how it used to be long, long ago.

How well I remember my own Mama getting up at four o'clock on those December mornings to do her baking, and I am sure she never thought of it as a curse. To her it was an exciting time, filled with fun and an eagerness to begin.

"How many kinds of cookies will you bake this Christmas?" one housewife would ask another.

And the answer would come: "This year I am baking only seventeen kinds of cookies and a *mjuk pepparkaka*."

And another wife would proudly proclaim, "This year I am baking twenty-nine kinds of cookies and *madelskorpor*."

Madelskorpor was a rusk with almonds in it and *mjuk pepparkaka* was a very special ginger cake. They, too, belonged to the Christmas baking, but they were not cookies and had to be classified in a separate category.

The housewives just loved to outdo each other when it came to the Christmas baking and the many varieties of cookies they could make. So in this early hour, when the smoke rose straight toward the sky from the tall chimney, busy hands were chopping nuts and orange peel and crunching sugar from the big sugar pyramid. Few thought of it as work. It was fun to make ready and bake the fancy creations for the household and the many guests that would visit during the gay holidays. Perhaps in their minds the housewives could already hear the sleigh bells outside and the eager feet stamping off snow on the doorstep, the firm knock at the front door and the hearty greetings. Then would come the time to fill the plates with cookies and fancy breads and to smell the aroma of coffee bubbling on the stove. That would be the time to sit and chat while the guests lingered long during those lazy days when little work needed to be done. They must have thought also of the wide, shining, blue eyes of the children as the goodies were placed in piles, one for each child. There would be one of every cooky, regardless of how many kinds had been baked. The mothers made the piles before going to church early on Christmas morning, and afterwards each child could eat to his heart's content. To make the family feel happy and important was the duty and responsibility of each housewife. It was her task! It was her joy! That was what she lived for. And most important was pleasing her husband who, after all, was the head of the household.

Yes, there was mixing and scraping and beating, the spreading of jams and perserves. No matter how meager the household budget, at Christmas time there was no skimping. Everything that went into the baking must be the finest quality. That was a *must* for this once-a-year cooky spree. Busy fingers cut and shaped the many doughs into breathtaking creations. There was always the traditional Christmas Buck, commemorating the ancients' worship of Tor, the god of strength and thunder, who had ridden through the skies with his two great bucks. There were also Christmas angels and stars in honor of Bethlehem; and, of course, the Santa Clauses made in the image of our own beloved *Tomte*. Christmas logs and half-moons, oak leaves and rings, S-shaped cookies and braided wreaths, and many, many more began to emerge on the baking trays. The Bucks and Santas were made large enough to hang on the Christmas tree, as were the gingerbread mamas and papas.

But before the actual baking took place, the stove had to be completely cleaned and the kitchen had to be spotless. No person other than the housewife could be in the kitchen during the baking time. This tradition was freely broken in our parsonage, and it had loosened up in many homes despite the dark omens. I was allowed to help Mama and to arise when she did in the early morning, perhaps because I was such a persistent child.

Oh, to capture again, just for one moment, the feeling that tingled through me when on a certain morning in dark December a familiar aroma drifted to my nostrils, penetrating my deep slumber. It was different from anything else in the whole world—the aroma of cookies baking in the kitchen. I knew then that Christmas was not far away, because at no other time did Mama bake cookies at that hour of the morning.

I counted on her good nature when I went against the rules and entered the kitchen. First, I would stand a few seconds outside the door; then I would push it open ever so slowly. Peeking in, I would get my first glimpse of Mama rushing about in her own kingdom. She would be rosy-cheeked and starry-eyed, humming softly the tune of a morning hymn. There was always a speck of flour on the tip of her nose, and invariably she would smile at me. How I loved to go from one pile of cookies to the next. They were all over the kitchen, in every available space, like little mountains, each more beautiful than the one before. After some hesitation, Mama would let me help, and to be trusted with placing the cookies in the tins was the most wonderful experience that could come to a young girl. They had to be handled as carefully as the thinnest crystal or china; they were that brittle. And to break one would be a terrible crime. So I lifted them, one by one; Mama had taught me to handle her creations just so.

The *Finska Bröd* were my favorites. I called them the miracle cookies. I loved to watch Mama's skillful hands mix the flour-crumbs into a smooth dough, which she would roll into yard lengths, no wider than her ring finger. She cut them into right-size pieces, a couple of inches long, brushed them with egg white that had been beaten into a fluff; then they were carefully dipped in coarse sugar and nuts which had been finely chopped. They always cracked on the top a little when they baked, as though they were bursting with goodness.

I did try once to measure Mama's "so much of this and so much of that," although she said it was easier to remember. You just took twice as much flour as butter, and the same in tablespoons of sugar as in cups of flour. So measuring it out, it came out something like this:

FINSKA BRÖD

2 cups butter	4 tablespoons sugar
(washed thoroughly)	1 teaspoon almond flavoring
4 cups flour	

Mix and work together until a smooth dough is formed. Roll into finger size lengths and cut into two-inch pieces. Brush with beaten egg white and dip into coarse sugar and finely chopped nuts. Bake at about 400 degrees until light brown.

This made a great many cookies and half the recipe is enough for the average family.

This morning baking would continue until all the cookies had been put away. The rest of the baking had to wait until nearer Christmas, to be fresh for day-before-Christmas afternoon coffee.

Then again the early-morning baking would begin. The yeast dough was set at night so that it would be ready to bake in the morning. It was bundled up in a woolen blanket or towels to keep it warm, and sometimes newspapers were wrapped around the blanket.

The rye bread was baked first. There was a special *vurt limpa* for Christmas made with syrup and delicious spices. It was made into many loaves, some round and some flat, to be used for the dipping-in-the-pot at noon of Christmas Eve. I can remember Mama taking the beautiful loaves out of the oven and how the aroma filled the whole house with Christmas fragrance. She brushed them quickly with syrup-water to make them shiny. Sometimes the flatbread was mixed with wheat flour to make it look extra light.

The coffee bread was made with lavish amounts of sugar and butter. There were long braided loaves, little round twisted buns, and the pretzel-shaped ones called *kringlor*. But I liked the *klipp krans* best. And how I loved to watch Mama make them!

Klipp krans was just coffee-bread dough that was rolled out flat like a cookie dough, then spread with lots of butter and sprinkled with sugar. Sometimes it would be spread with almond paste or preserves or raisins and nuts—whatever suited the cook at the time. Then it was rolled into a ring, large or small, according to the size of the family. Ours was always a great big one! Then it would be cut with the scissors all across its top. The baker just snipped and cut any old way. After it had risen to twice its original size, it was brushed with egg white and sprinkled with coarse sugar and slivered almonds. It was baked in a moderate oven and proved to be the choicest of all coffee bread. Or maybe I feel that way because of my childhood memories.

Now if a wife wanted to be really fancy in her baking, she would make, in addition to all the other breads, some *Viener bröd*. This was a Danish pastry, and it had to be made on the morning of the day before Christmas because it tasted good only if it was newly baked. What a treat to have *Viener bröd* for early-morning coffee!

Mama would take

> 3 cups flour
> ½ cup sugar
> 1 egg
> A piece of yeast (two yeast cakes)
> 1 cup milk
> ½ lb. butter

She would dump the flour onto the baking board in a heap and make a hole in the middle. Into this hole she would break the egg, crumble the yeast cakes and pour in the sugar. Then, spilling a small amount of milk into the mixture, she would stir it slowly with a fork, adding a little more milk from time to time until it was all mixed in. Then she would sprinkle more flour on the board and roll the dough flat with a rolling pin. She would spread it with butter, and fold it over and over until the butter was all rolled in. Then she would cut it into strips and twist them to make pretzel-shaped buns. She would then let them rise to twice their size, and bake them in a hot oven (400 degrees) until they were light brown. As soon as they came out of the oven, they were spread with a paste made of two tablespoons of milk and two tablespoons of powdered sugar. This hardened into a lovely glaze and made a pastry fit for a queen to eat at any time.

That was Christmas baking as I remember it from my own "once-upon-a-time." There was a certain mystery about it and an excitement different from anything else in a child's mind. In it the good of the land was shared in the togetherness of family life. After all, didn't the baking ingredients come from the crops, from the fields that in the fall were heavy with grain? It tied together like a beautiful wreath all the things that belonged to Christmas, and tradition was the big red bow that put the finishing touch on all the work.

The *Så-Kaka,* the sowing loaf, was a very special

bread, always baked at Christmas time. It contained all the goodness which could be put into it, and sometimes it was a mixture of many kinds of flour. It was a big round loaf not to be eaten, but to be saved for spring when the sowing took place. Sometimes the loaf was reduced to fine crumbs and mixed with the seeds, and sometimes it was broken into pieces and plowed right into the earth. It was believed that this would bring blessings and good luck to the soil in which the seed was sown and that it would mean a prosperous harvest. Faithfully, year after year, generation after generation, the farm people lovingly and generously prepared this loaf of bread that would bring joy and prosperity and blessings.

I am sorry to think that the years have destroyed this tradition, that our modern times have erased the value of it. Now the only remembrance of it and many others is in the stories told of how it used to be when the welfare of the home and loved ones meant more to people than anything else in the world.

THREE

IN THE dark ages when Sweden was a heathen country, long, long before the light of the child of Bethlehem began to shine on the world, the pig was a sacred animal to Frö, the goddess of plenty. It was believed then that if a pig was slaughtered according to heathen ritual, the vitality that had once been his would enter into the person who ate of his flesh and would give him an enormous amount of strength and health.

The ritual slaughtering had to take place before the dawn. Oaths were solemnly sworn as the pig's life ebbed away with the blood which left his body from the deep gash in his throat. Strong liquor was poured over his back; and if a person dipped a finger into the blood and made a mark on his own forehead, good luck would follow in the months ahead.

At the Festival of Lights, the pig was a most important animal, roasted and devoured by the people, who ate and drank beyond their usual capacity. The tradition of eating too much at Christmas time has stayed on with the Swedish people, for at no other season of the year is more food or drink consumed. And the pig has remained the favorite dish for the feast days.

The pig which had the honor of becoming a glorified Christmas pig was chosen very shortly after its birth. Selected as a tiny piglet, he was then pampered and fed the best of food, so his meat would be of the finest quality. Not everybody was lucky enough to have a farm, but almost every family had a Christmas pig, which was boarded on a farm from the spring of his birth until October when his days on earth were ended.

It was usually on a Saturday in the spring that the parents would take their family to a nearby farm and buy a little piglet; then they would board him there during his short life span. The piglet selected would have to be perfect, rosy and round with tiny ears, a long pink snout, and a curly little tail. He always made a grunting sound and he was always hungry. He was the children's delight from the beginning; and in the months that followed, he became their pet. They loved him and gave him such names as Oscar, Steffan, or Amandus. This name he soon acknowledged when he was called, especially if food was brought to his sty. He would climb the boards with his cloven hoofs and squeal with joy when anyone approached with a pail of food, mostly potatoes, milk, and table scraps.

Petted and coddled, he soon became big and fat. Toward the end of the summer, he could hardly make it to the trough where he ate, and he could no longer climb the boards. His stomach almost touched the floor when he waddled around, and he became too lazy to move at all, except to eat.

Every time the children came to visit their pet, he had grown fatter and he slept most of the time in the plentiful straw that had been provided for him in great abundance in the corner of his sty. At first he loved to play with it and get both the straw and himself covered with dirt. But by the middle of October he had become too big and fat to move. He only made a grunting noise in answer to the children's call, and they knew that it was just too much of an effort for him to come to the boards so they could pet him.

Then suddenly it would happen! That father of the house would announce: "Amandus is big enough now. We shall ask Farmer Svenson when we can have him slaughtered!"

How well I can remember Papa uttering those words to us children, and what a stab of pain went through my heart. How we pleaded for mercy for our pet, Amandus; but our pleas fell on deaf ears. Since this repeated itself every year, Papa had learned to harden his heart every October. Amandus had to be sacrificed for our holiday food. With a red apple in his mouth, he was destined to become a decorative Christmas-table centerpiece. We realized that Papa's love for Amandus had not been the unselfish love that ours was, and that nothing in the whole world could save our friend from being put to death.

We children did not go to the farm that Saturday. Mama went though, I remember, to be of help. Some-one had to stir flour into the pig's blood as he was stuck with the cruel knife. We all sat in the parsonage kitchen, sad and hurt, looking at the hands of the clock on the wall, wondering if Amandus' hour had come. In our minds we could hear our pet's cries, but we were powerless to help him. Every fall we lived through the same thing, and hundreds of other children suffered as we did. At that time we all vowed among ourselves that never again would we accept a little piglet as a pet. But when springtime came, we had forgotten what the end would be and the reason that Papa bought the piglet for us.

The darkest day of our lives passed. The pig was butchered into many pieces and put down in brine to keep until December when he would serve the purpose for which he was born, to be a Christmas pig.

What a busy time was late December. Most of the baking was finished. Instead of the aroma of cookies baking, the kitchen was filled with the odor of meat cooking and the mixture of delicious and mysterious spices, used only at this time of the year. The two big hams were rosy red. As a rule, only one was used for Christmas; the other one was saved for later in the year. The ham was decorated in a special way for Christmas Eve. There was colored fringed tissue paper surrounding it and some curly green parsley that was grown in a flowerpot to be used on this special occasion.

Parts of the pig, like the lungs and heart, were boiled and then ground and mixed with barley and spices. This *pölsa*, fried on Christmas Day for breakfast, was one of my favorite dishes. How good it tasted when we returned home from church! It was served with *blod-palt*, a wonderful blood pudding that we ate with lingon berries. Any remaining *pölsa* was made into *hacke-korv*, which was a sausage. We stuffed the mixture into the skins by hand. The skins, too, were a part of the pig that had been cleaned at the time of the

37

slaughtering and kept in salt water until they were white and clear and ready for use.

There were many kinds of sausages besides the *hacke-korv*. There was *fläsk-korv*, made with pork meat and spices. And the *koke-korv* made with beef and pork; and the *potatis-korv* was beef and pork and potatoes mixed together, each with the mysterious spices that set it apart from any other. The sausage ropes were cut into the desired sizes and tied at both ends with white string. One had to be careful not to stuff them too full, lest they burst when they were boiled.

At least two different kinds of headcheese were made. One, of ground veal and pork hardened in a fine mold, was called *kalvsylta*. Then there was one called *press-sylta*, made in layers of pork and veal with coarsely chopped pepper and salt on each layer. This was wrapped in pork rind, tied with strings, placed in brine, and a heavy weight was laid on it. Sliced very thinly for Christmas Eve it was delicious.

How much food a big pig could provide for one family! There were the pork loins and the spareribs and the liver, all contributing wonderful meals for holiday feasting. The salted side meat, a mixture of lean and fat, we sliced like bacon. The liver was divided and some of it was made into liverwurst. But the largest portion was cooked slowly all day on top of the stove after having been specked with suet. Served with a rich brown gravy it contributed to an elegant meal.

Every bit of the pig was used for food. The pigs' feet, a Christmas Eve delicacy, had been in brine for weeks and were boiled and eaten with pickled beets. Some of the blood of the pig was used for blood bread, *palt-bröd*. It was left to dry hard and then boiled and eaten with a thick white sauce. It kept all winter long and was a real treat. The kidneys, too, were especially good, fried in their own special way with onions.

The pig was a blessing, and nothing could have taken its place in a Swedish household. As far back as the records go, there has always been a pig to feed and gladden each household in those cold, dark Swedish Decembers. And no matter how modernized Yule customs become, there will always be a Christmas Pig!

FOUR

THE CHRISTMAS house cleaning had nothing to do with the annual fall cleaning. There was no connection. This was a ritual set apart and was an intrinsic part of the Christmas preparations. Never was there another operation like it! Out came the soap and the rags and the brushes, and you set to work. Each room was gone over from top to bottom. There was not one corner of the house, from the cellar to the attic, that was not thoroughly cleaned. The old traditions had instituted this cleaning-before-Christmas, and I am sure that it will always remain with and belong to Sweden.

In heathen times, there was a belief that at this time of year in the cold darkness, goblins and giants and trolls and various evil beings drew near to people's homes without being seen. They had the power to throw evil spells over entire households. Even in the Christian times some of these superstitions still hung over the people and the goblins in particular were feared especially at Christmas time when they liked to exchange their own children for human babies. The sad part of such ignorance was that a child who grew up with an abnormally large head, or one mentally retarded, was believed to be a goblin-baby, a changeling. Even if a child was naughtier than other children, or unusually mischievous, adults would often cry out during exceptionally trying times, "I believe you are a goblin-child!"

But it was said that evil monsters had a dread fear of cleanliness. And if a house were completely clean, without a speck of dirt anywhere, they would be completely powerless and their bewitching would have no effect on their intended victims. And because the people believed that evil was strong at Christmas time, but that good was stronger, they used cleanliness as a weapon, like a disinfectant, to rid themselves of the threat of evil spells. Never were dirt and dust and cobwebs more hunted than at Christmas-cleaning time.

Curtains and drapes came down, and rugs and quilts and blankets and bedclothes were shaken and aired out of doors until they could be brought in fresh and free from dust. Every bit of furniture was moved from its place so that no dust or dirt could hide from the eye of the cleaner, not even in the dark corners of the house. Nothing went unmoved or undetected. Windowpanes were washed until they were sparkling and clear, and ceilings and walls were brushed down. Even the large wooden floors were scrubbed on hands and knees until they showed gleaming stretches between the gaily colored hand-woven rag rugs.

The starched lace curtains competed in whitness with the deep snow outside the window. And when every drawer, every closet, every nook was spotless and in order, the house began to take on a holiday look.

The silver and copper shone their brightest. Mama never used silver polish to perform this miracle; perhaps there was no silver polish in those days. She used wood-ash, with a little water, which soon removed the blackest tarnish from any silver. But often the pieces were simply placed in a bowl of warm soapsuds, scrubbed with a soft brush, and wiped dry. And there they were—trying to outshine the December sun as they were placed on the embroidered cloth on the serving table in the best room where the big round table stood in the middle of the floor.

But perhaps the kitchen showed the greatest signs of cleaning. There was a certain hominess about the large Swedish kitchen with all its copperware spread out on walls and stoves and shelves. The big copper coffeepots shone like gold and the sheen of the copper reservoir at the side of the black iron stove made a fine contrast. On the broad window sills red geraniums in full bloom added a touch of bright color to the scene. It was as though everything wanted to sparkle cheerfully, for the gay days ahead.

The housewife herself moved with a certain grace as she went about her tasks. Her heart was light now that most of the work had been accomplished. It was hard work, but very gratifying to behold the results.

The children had all taken part in the work. They had been free from school for their winter vacation since the early part of December. Each member of the family wanted a share in making the home Christmas-ready and took great pride in each job he was allowed to perform. I often wonder how dark, threatening thoughts could get a foothold in such a happy family atmosphere, but certain superstitions seemed to be a strong chain with which some people's minds were bound. Nevertheless, the work kept the children busy and the grownups content.

Little was done during the holidays, and one of the last tasks to be completed was to see that plenty of wood was chopped and placed in the big wood bin in the kitchen and that extra logs were stacked in the back hall. It was believed that with the last armload of wood, *Julsvennen*, a strange-looking, imaginary creature entered the house and took his place under the dining-room table. He had only one large eye in the middle of his forehead, but he could see everything that went on. We could not see him, but we knew he was there. If the household was filled with joy and harmony, there was nothing to fear from him. But if there was trouble between members of the family, awful things would begin to take place immediately, and there would be no luck for that family in the coming year.

The Christmas bath, the night before Christmas Eve, was the last item of the pre-holiday ritual and was also traditional. Out came the old wooden tub! It was placed right in the middle of the kitchen floor and filled with steaming hot water. And beginning with the youngest, each person had his turn until each member of the family was properly scrubbed and worthy to dwell in a spotless house. For on the morning of the day before Christmas everything had to be perfectly clean and beautiful.

You awoke that morning wiith a deep feeling of exhilaration, acutely aware that all was in order. And then began the longest wait of a child's life—the eternal period of time until Christmas was really there.

FIVE

ALONG with the baking and cleaning and general preparations, there were Christmas gifts to be taken care of. These special gifts, given on Christmas Eve, presented a very minor problem in those days and were but a small part of the Christmas festivities.

The Swedish Christmas giving started out as a joke. The gifts were called *Julklappar*. *Klapp* means to knock and people would make silly things, and on

Christmas Eve would knock on the door of a friend or neighbor, throw a gift into the house, and run. There are many stories based about this sort of giving, which soon broadened into another channel. The children of long ago were led to believe that the god Tor's bucks brought the gifts to the household. And as a symbol of this, bucks, big and small, were made out of straw. They became so popular that, though the belief was discarded, the bucks lived on. And even in this age, if you travel to Sweden at Christmas time, you will see Christmas bucks brought out as decorations. They are sold to people everywhere.

It was much later that the *Tomte* was given the honor of coming around with a big sack of gifts on his back on Christmas Eve. He always walked. He walked hundreds and hundreds of miles; and although Sweden is the land of the reindeer, there was never even a rumor that he drove one, or that reindeer had anything to do with Christmas. It was believed, however, that only good children received gifts. The naughty ones were left only a stick with which they were to be spanked. So, of course, all children were especially careful to be on their good behavior before Christmas, although the *Tomte* watched them throughout the whole year.

Although the gifts, as a rule, were given out on Christmas Eve, each family followed its own pattern. We children had our very own experience in Christmas giving. I am sure that Papa wanted to teach us a lesson that would be valuable all through life. He wanted us to learn that it was not the price of the gift that counted, but rather the spirit in which it was given. It is hard to believe that Papa on the twenty-third of December gave to each of us eight children only fifty *öre*. And with that meager sum we were to buy gifts for nine family members. We were not prompted as to what we should give; this was to be our own decision. We were in complete control of our money.

As I think back I can see now that sweet woman who managed the variety store on the hill in our town. She stood patiently behind her counter and waited on people busy with Christmas shopping. When the eight children from the parsonage entered, searching, asking, trying to find the best possible Christmas presents, what ever did she think, I wonder, of Papa, the village pastor, giving each child such a small sum to buy with? But she was wonderful in helping us. We would end up with something like a bright collar button for Papa; a spool of number 40 thread for Mama; and for our brothers and sisters—a barrette, a pencil, a pad of paper, an eraser, a ribbon, a blotter, and a red crayon.

It took us about one hour to do our shopping. Every penny had to be spent carefully, but we made it at last. Happier children than we, tramping home in the snow that afternoon, couldn't be found anywhere in Sweden. We hugged our brown bags close to us as each contained gifts which had to be wrapped and labeled. We knew nothing about fancy gift wrappings; at home we found paper, brown or gray, or even nice newspaper. But each gift was wrapped and tied as carefully and with as much pride and tenderness as if it were worth hundreds of *kronor*. We wrote with ink on the paper, using our very best penmanship.

> To my lovely Mama
> From her eldest daughter

and so on down through the long line of names.

What fun it was and what excitement! I have never since wrapped a gift as meaningful as that spool of number 40 thread so long, long ago. The gifts, wrapped and labeled, were given to Mama to keep until Christmas Eve when they turned up again in the strangest way.

I know now that this Christmas-gift buying was fine training, a great heritage planted in our hearts and minds. And although Papa and Mama gave each of us additional larger gifts, nothing could equal those small ones which we ourselves chose and wrapped and which played such a big part in our Christmas happiness. Perhaps no one can understand how much secret whispering there was behind closed doors, or with what wide-eyed wonder we anticipated the opening of the gifts. The big day was just around the corner now, but the waiting period that remained seemed the longest children had ever endured.

On the afternoon of the tweny-third, Papa, like hundreds of other fathers all over the country, took his children into the woods to find a Christmas tree.

The tradition of the Christmas tree was given to us by our neighbor, Germany, where it originated way back in 1600. In Sweden the idea was taken up by the nobility in 1740 and was passed on to the common people in the 1800's. But it took root very quickly and solidly and has been loved and practiced each Christmas since.

To me, it was one of the most beautiful of all traditions. That hour of tramping in the deep snow of the woods, looking among the beautiful spruces for *the one* was a time of happy excitement. The snow-covered trees looked like lovely brides standing there in the silence of the green forest. We walked and walked into the very heart of the woodland. Here and there a bird would fly up, frightened by our invasion. In the snow there were prints of the fox and the rabbit, and sometimes even of a deer or an elk. I can see Papa now, an ax over his shoulder, leading the long line of children. Then suddenly there came through the forest the echo of someone's chopping far, far away; some lucky family had found their tree.

Papa was very critical. Some of the trees were too

bushy, some too short, some too tall, some too thin; the branches of others were not even. Never had Papa been more critical of our judgment. But finally the long-awaited words came: "I think we have found our Christmas tree. This spruce is just about perfect."

He would measure it with his eyes, looking it up and down, and we would stand there breathless, unable to move, just waiting. Finally Papa would lift the ax and then it was the sound of our tree-chopping that echoed through the woods.

We would brush the snow off of it as best we could. Then each of us would take hold of some part of it and begin our long, happy walk home. It was really going to be Christmas now; nothing could confirm that fact better than carrying home the Christmas tree.

That particular night all over Sweden there were mysterious goings-on. Behind closed doors all the things for decorating the tree were assembled. They had been put away in boxes or drawers and in our house only Papa knew where they were kept. On a tray were the bucks and the rest of the decorations made from the gingerbread dough and strung with new white strings. The figures had eyes of raisins and the plump little men had red buttons of sugar candy on their coats. The angels were white and glossy with sugar frosting. On another tray lay the tassel candy, wrapped in fringed tissue paper, and the *confect*, a candy especially made for the tree and always bought in the store. The small white candles were there, just enough of them, and red apples to hang beneath and balance each candle. We always had real candles, and no one ever thought of the possibility of fire. I never remember one tree burning up when I was a child in Sweden.

The night before Christmas Eve everything had to be in order. The scene had to be set because on the twenty-fourth we had to wake up to a perfect house, shiny and beautiful, to go with the joy and sparkle in our hearts. And that night we dreamed about the big shining Christmas star and the gifts and the parties and the fun and play and laughter and gladness everywhere. To live through it hour by hour, sleeping to pass the time, and not trying to hurry each minute was the hardest thing we had to do. But we knew that when we awoke to the early-morning noises in the kitchen that this day we had awaited so long would be the finest day of all the year.

SIX

How vividly it comes to me now, as I dream back into the long ago, the feeling that came to us when we opened our eyes on the morning of the day before Christmas, *Julafton* in Swedish. The very word has a jubilant ring to it. It was *Julafton* all over Sweden and you awoke to a spotless world, a truly happy world!

In the days of long, long ago, on that special morning the whole family would gather at the front door, which the head of the house would open wide. He would stand quietly for a moment, and then in a loud voice would call out into the beautiful, snow-covered wonderland, "Welcome, dear Christmas!"

This was the morning when the sheaf for the birds was set out. That tradition is still observed, and I predict that it will always be among the Swedish people. Each household in olden days tried to set its sheaf a little higher than its neighbor's. It was believed that the family which could set its sheaf the highest would be the luckiest one in the approaching year. So the farmers used to get long poles and raise the sheaves up on them high into the air.

In my time, however, it was placed outside the kitchen window, and there was no competition involved. It was there as a feast for the many birds that would come for their Christmas treat, but also so we could have the pleasure of watching them. They were so beautiful, especially the *Domherrar* in their red vests and the black and white *Skata*. The *Skata* was a bird that stole things; and in the summer time you had to be careful not to leave any silver around. They very quickly picked up any spoon or fork and took it to their nests in the tall oak trees. They were very large birds and very clever. But in the winter, you accepted this sneaky thief with the rest, and it was fun to see them all so close by and to admire their beauty.

There were many, many different kinds of birds.

They came in flocks for their feast, and what a picture they made in that large yellow sheaf, bursting with grain, against a background of snow-covered fir trees. What a twittering noise they made, and what a commotion as they celebrated their Christmas holiday.

It wasn't just the birds that were taken care of on that day. All the farm animals were given a special treat. There were oats and lumps of sugar for the horses and there was extra hay for the cows. The pigs got boiled potatoes and skim milk with their mush, and the chickens were given lots of the very best grain. Cats received a bowl of cream; and dogs, a big bone with lots of meat on it. The children were usually given the pleasure of taking care of the Christmas feed for the animals, and each animal was wished a *God Jul* (Merry Christmas). So Christmas cheer was spread everywhere on that blessed day.

During the forenoon, as a rule, the Christmas tree which had been brought home the previous day was decorated. Each Swedish home had its own tradition as to who was given this honor. But in our parsonage, it was always Papa who did the decorating, and we children had no part in it. His Papa had always done it in their home, and his Papa before him; and in that same way, traditions were passed down and formed patterns in the different homes across the land.

We children had to wait outside the door of the best room where most of the Christmas festivities would take place. It was a long wait on a long day. The hours ticked away so slowly; and when we heard Papa's feet moving about, we could visualize the beauty that we would soon behold. Papa was very systematic, and we were sure that he had a ruler and measured the distance between each candle, making sure that the balancing apples hung at exactly the same angle. But presently, the door would open and there it would stand, the tree of trees, our very own selection, in all its glory. And we were sure that ours was the most beautiful *Julgran* (Christmas tree) in all of Sweden.

It was the busiest day of the year for the house-wives, while the rest of the family had very little to take up their time. But the mother had to prepare the *smörgåsbord* and all the other courses for the big feast, now only hours away. The house was clean; there had only been a little last-minute dusting to do that morning. Beds and dishes had been done quickly, and now the thing to which she gave all her time was fixing the food.

The first chore, perhaps, was putting the rice porridge on the stove. It had to boil very, very slowly all day long in order to be just right. Every so often it was stirred, and a little more milk might be added to it. In the later hours, a large stick of whole cinnamon was placed in the white fluffy mixture, and, of course, the traditional whole almond. The almond was very important because if you were a bachelor or a spinster, and if you got the almond in your porridge on Christmas Eve, it was absolutely certain that you would be married before the *Julafton* came again.

The next thing to be put on the stove was the big kettle that left little room for other kettles. It contained the pig's head and feet, a piece of beef, and lots of sausages. All this would simmer slowly all morning until noon when the dipping party took place.

The Dip-in-the-Pot, or in Swedish *doppa i grytan,* was strictly a family affair, carried on in Swedish households for as long as any one has a record. The tradition seems ageless, and it is very dear to the people's hearts because this is a custom that is their very own, the one that sets them apart from all other countries.

This is a kitchen celebration and the table usually stands in the center of the room, covered with a snowy white linen cloth. The plates are in a pile with the silver forks beside them. There are drinking glasses on the table, one for each person. There is a large pitcher of foaming Christmas ale and an enormous tray filled with homemade Christmas bread. The aroma which fills the kitchen suggests only one thing—CHRISTMAS! There is on the table a plate laden with chunks of sausage and slices of meat, but the rest of the things in the kettle are left there to continue simmering slowly for the evening meal.

In many Swedish homes, stronger drinks appear at this time to help keep people happy during the long wait. But in our home, as in many hundreds of others, that was taboo. We were happy anyway and needed no stimulant to make us so.

And as the pale December sun sent its rays through the shining windowpanes with their crisp white curtains, the father of the house picked up his plate, speared a chunk of limpa bread on his fork, filled his glass with the beverage so it would be ready upon his return, and started the march toward the stove. The family followed according to age; and if there was a baby, the mother who came last in line would carry him so that all the family participated. The father stopped at the big kettle and dipped his bread into the broth and then circled back to the table. He helped himself to meat from the platter, took his glass, and sat down wherever he chose to. The rest of the family followed his every move to the last detail.

This meal was very special, and there was only one rule for all to observe—not to eat too much. There must be room for the food that would be served at dinner, for that was the biggest meal of all the year. But there was always a very festive feeling at day-before-Christmas noontime, and family members were gay and gentle with each other. I don't remember that there was ever a spanking or even a harsh word spoken.

As I recall it, a little before the noon hour all the

stores closed and the activities in the town stopped. Only skeleton forces remained in places which had to be attended. All minds were centered around just one thing, home and family. It seemed that for a time the world stood still, waiting for the great night which was drawing nearer and nearer.

The day seemed to go on forever; there was no end in sight. But the mother, the only one rushing and running, perhaps wished the day had twice as many hours when there was so much to get ready.

In the middle of the afternoon, the family gathered again in the kitchen. This was time for coffee and cooky-tasting. Only a few kinds of cookies were set out along with some of the fancy coffee bread. After all, it would not be fair to place too many temptations in front of an appetite which had to be saved. Each person helped himself, but with the same warning echoing again and again, "Don't eat too much!" You just had to be hungry when you went to the table that night.

It grew dark early. A little after two in the afternoon the sun began to go down and dusk settled over the countryside. At three o'clock the lamps had to be lit.

As evening approached, quick feet ran back and forth from the kitchen to the best room, and exciting odors tickled the nostrils. The table was set now, the big table with all the leaves in it. It almost filled the whole room. Again there appeared a lovely white linen cloth and some green boughs from the spruce, tall candles on either side of the large friendly pig head, blushing there in the middle of everything with a large red apple in his mouth. Linen napkins, which had assumed the unique shape of a fan or a flower, stood beside each plate. An artist had set that table, an artist who had done this year after year from the time she had married and moved into the house. Each year some little touch of her own was added to the beauty, but she was always very careful not to disrupt the pattern of the traditions which had come down from the generations before her. With these she would never dare to tamper.

Suddenly there came a strong pungent odor from the kitchen. It was the Christmas fish, the *lutfisk*, cooking. This was a strange food belonging strictly to Christmas. It had been bought in the fall in long dry sticks which were put into a strong lime solution until they began to take on the right substance and again look like fish. About a week before Christmas they were placed in a tub of clear, cold water which was changed more and more often as the day drew nearer until the fish was ready to be boiled. It was a fluffy, snow-white food, appetizing to the eye, but when it began to boil, sharply biting to the nose. Most of the time it had to be cooked in a cheesecloth or it would have boiled away into nothingness.

But we did not mind the odor. To us Swedes it meant Christmas Eve, and it was loved and welcomed. The fish was served with a thick, smooth white sauce, made with lots of butter and milk and with a bit of heavy cream added to make it extra good and rich. Without the *lutfisk*, it would not be Christmas Eve in Sweden.

Finally the hour was upon us! It was time to take our places at the Christmas table, so beautifully arranged in every detail. Each dish was decorated in an unusual way, one outdoing the other. There it was, the traditional *smörgåsbord*, in front of our very eyes:

Sliced Christmas bread, flatbread, and hard bread
Butter in fancy rolls, decorated with curly green parsley
Plain cheese, *bondost*, goatcheese, cummingcheese
Pickled herring, salt raw herring with chives
Sill in gaffelbitar (another herring), anchovies
Herring salad (in Swedish, *sill-salad*)
Pickled beets, pickled Swedish cucumber
Dill pickles
Spareribs with applesauce
Pig's feet
Jellied headcheese
Rolled headcheese
Stuffed eggs
Small meatballs
Sardines
Asparagus omelet
Lingonberries

Fish pudding with melted butter
  Anchovies and smelts casserole
    Rolled fish fillets with lemon sauce
      Brown beans
        Sausages: boiled, smoked, hot and cold
          Christmas ham

But before we began to eat, Papa opened the big family Bible which had a special place on the table and he read the old Christmas story. Then he bowed his head in thankfulness as did Mama and all eight children. Papa's prayer went out for the whole world, and then came the Amen.

Our eyes almost popped out of our heads looking at so much goodness, and we could eat all we wanted. Since there were so many of us, this did not happen every day in our home. But on this night we made up for it. We filled our plates to overflowing over and over.

The second course was the *lutfisk*, which we ate with little boiled potatoes. The fish went down slowly, for it had to be boned before the sauce was put on it. It shook on our plates and needed lots of salt and coarse pepper to flavor it. The fork turned black just from touching it, and I wondered, in later years, what happened to the lining of our stomachs. But we Swedes are a hardy race, and I never knew of anyone whose health was affected by eating the fish.

Then came the rice porridge, white and sweet, especially after we had put cinnamon and sugar on it and topped it with plenty of milk and cream. But before we could eat this tempting dish, each of us had to make up a rhyme. This was fun and added much laughter to the meal.

There were many stories connected with this tradition of rhyming over the rice. There were times when it served as a reminder to someone who had made a promise and had failed to keep it. It must not sound mean, but still the person involved must get the hint that the promise was still remembered. And so the rhyme might go something like this:

> A coat was promised me last year.
> It must be mighty big I fear,
>   Or else too small or wide to fit.
>   A promise is so very cheap.
>   It costs us only if we keep.
>   So I ask again where is it?

Such rhymes were usually recited in families where the children were fairly grown up. In our family group we resolved to say just a few lines with no particular reason or meaning so long as they rhymed.

> This wonderful rice is delicious and sweet,
> The lady who cooked it just can't be beat.

When the Christmas rice is eaten, be kind,
Or I surely will give you a piece of my mind.

These rhymes went all around the table from the oldest to the youngest; and if one was too young, there was always help from the elders:

Good, good rice.
Mama so nice.

It wasn't hard at all, and it surely produced gay conversation and laughter around our table.

Then what fun we had with the almond. If we had with us as a guest that night a lady who was still unmarried, we tried our best to see that the nut landed in her plate. Then our happiness knew no bounds, for we were sure that by the next Christmas she would be cooking her own rice for her own husband.

After the rice porridge came cold savory fruit soup. But by then we were so full that it was hard to eat more than a spoonful. We did our best, however, as this was also a very special dish, just filled with prunes and cherries, apples and pears, and other fruits. But one could only eat so much; even if the will was there, one's appetite had limits. And we had to tell ourselves there would be other days and be content to let the meal end.

Never were dishes cleared away so quickly! Mama put the food away while the rest of us helped to clean up. Soon the table was set again for coffee, which we would have a little later, after the gifts. When all was ready, we entered the best room again to take our places and gaze at the lovely Christmas tree with its live white candles burning so lovely and still. Just at that moment a message came for Papa. Someone in the parish was ill and needed him and he had to leave as was his obligation.

A few minutes later there came a firm knock on the front door, and Mama hurried to open it. Our hearts stood still for a breathless moment, and then we heard Mama say, "Come in! Come in, Mr. *Tomte*."

Then in he came, big and round as if he was padded. He bounced right in with snow on his boots, but dressed in a very strange way. I could have sworn he wore Papa's red bathrobe and the stocking hat with the long tassel was just like the one my little sister had. But we children never wondered out loud about such things. Anything could happen at Christmas. It was a time filled with mysteries one could not understand, and wasn't Christmas Eve itself a great miracle?

Mama spoke kindly to the *Tomte* and asked him questions.

"How far have you walked today, Mr. *Tomte*?" . .

"Oh, I have walked hundreds and hundreds of miles, tramping all over the land to find good children. Have you any good children in this house?"

"Oh, yes, yes," said Mama. "All of our children—all eight of them are very, very good."

For a moment we had been a little frightened that Mama would remember moments when we had not been so good. But she had forgotten those times, and we were happy and relieved.

The *Tomte* sat right down on the floor and crossed his legs. Then he took the sack from his back. He opened it wide—what do you think?—he began to take out the very packages we had wrapped the night before. How in the world could they have gotten into his sack? Again we didn't try to figure it out; we took what he gave us and made little piles of our gifts and one for our absent Papa, hoping he would get back while the *Tomte* was still there. But Papa did not come, and the *Tomte* was in a hurry, for he had many more stops to make. We followed him to the door, bowing and curt-seying and saying thank you many, many times. We promised to be good so he would come back again next year.

It was fun to tell Papa all about it when he came home only minutes later. He sat down and began to open his gifts, and we all hoped that next year he could be home when the miracle of the *Jul-Tomte* happened.

After we had coffee, it was right to bed for us because the morrow was an important day, too, and we all had to leave for church very early in the morning. There would hardly be time to close our eyes before we would have to get up again. . . . The minute we lay down, we fell fast asleep. What a day it had been! We were so grateful and so happy and felt so good and warm inside, knowing that we had had the best Christmas Eve in the whole world.

SEVEN

CHRISTMAS DAY, following so close after Christmas Eve, was almost an anticlimax. It could have been a very dull day had it not been for the early-morning Christmas service. This in itself held so much excitement and beauty for us that it made the day well worth while. Before Christmas Eve there had been time-consuming hard work every moment of the day. People had been getting up early and going to bed late in order to get everything done. Now suddenly the work had stopped and during these blessed days time was used only to enjoy families, friends, and neighbors.

The service on Christmas Day was called *Jul-otta* in Swedish, words that have a very wonderful sound to us who know their full meaning. The *Jul-otta* definitely originated way back in Catholic Sweden and has been continued ever since those early years.

Early, early on Christmas Day the mother awakened her family. Sometimes it was as early as 4:30 A.M. that the members of the household had to leave their warm beds. But no one complained, for it was a joy to attend church on this particular morning, and no one would miss it for anything in the world.

Most people in the olden days liked to travel to church in a horse and sleigh, and the farmers were kind enough to pick up those who had no sleighs of their own. After coffee and coffee bread, the family was ready to start out under the star-studded, cold winter sky, and they waited for the jingle of the sleigh bells. What a lovely sound it was to the children's ears! And for some lucky child there was a flare to hold while standing on the little platform in back of the driver. When the others were bedded down under the fur rug, snug and comfortable, off they went through the snow.

Along the road they were joined by other sleighs and the bells on the horses made music on Christmas morning that was beautiful to hear. Then suddenly, there in the distance, stood the church with candles lighting all its windows and a big bright star gleaming over the door.

"Come!" sang the sleigh bells.

"Come!" sputtered the flares.

"Come!" called the church. "Come to worship the newborn king!"

There was a scramble to get the horses tied and the feed bags over their noses. No one would think of having his horse stand hungry on this blessed morning. The stars twinkled brightly as the people filed into the church welcomed by organ music and softly flickering candles.

When the church was filled with people, old and young, the first hymn was begun. And what a song it was! It swelled the rafters of the little church and drifted out, loud and clear, into the crisp December morning. It was an old hymn, one which was always sung on this particular morning, one that belonged to this day alone, and one that the people knew by heart. It would not have been Christmas without "We Hail Thee, Beautiful Morning, or in Swedish:

> Var hälsad sköna morningonstund
> Som av profeters helga mund
> Är oss bebådad vorden.
> Du stora dag,
> Du sälla dag,

På vilken himlens välbehag
Ännu besöker jorden.
Unga, sjunga
Med de gamla,
Sig församla
Jordens böner,
Kring den största of dess söner.

The people sang about Christmas morning, foretold
by the prophets of old, a great morning, a joyous morning, on which all heaven's blessings rest—when the
young sing with the old, and all earthly prayers are
gathered to present to the greatest of earth's sons.

The minister speaking from the platform at times
became a blur to the children's eyes. Their lids were
heavy as if weighted with sand and it became harder
and harder to keep them open.

"And the people who live in darkness shall see a
great light!" thundered the minister.

The candles flickered and the smoke from them
made people's eyes sting. The words from the pulpit
fell almost like hammer blows; it seemed the sermon
would never end. But presently it was over and the
congregation sang the last hymn and filed out into the
crisp, cold, dark morning. There was still no sign of
dawn, and it would be good to go home to food and
warmth.

But the people took time to shake hands and wish

each other a *God Jul* (Merry Christmas), and there were many invitations to visit in each other's homes. After all, that wonderful Christmas baking had to be eaten and enjoyed.

There were no flares on the way home, just the sleigh bells for the ride through the white snowy world. The horses did not run very fast, as it seemed there was no real hurry. Christmas Day seemed to have more hours than other days because we had begun it so much earlier.

There was no racing as in the old days when each farmer had tried to get home from church first in order to be blessed with luck for the coming year. But it hadn't been so long ago that there had been a great rush each Christmas after the early-morning church service. People believed that the farmer who could drive home the fastest would have the most plentiful crop the following year and would be especially blessed. Families almost threw themselves into the sleighs and the horses were given a crack of the whip to make them go their fastest from the start.

Like the wind they flew over the snow and many are the stories connected with the ride home from church on a Christmas morning. There were those who abandoned an overturned sleigh and came home on the back of the horse leaving their family to be picked up later. There were some who played tricks on their neighbors, tying up their horses or loosening the sleigh from the horse—anything to delay the other fellow. One could visualize how it used to be back in those lively days when everything connected with Christmas had a gain or loss to it in some way and each family looked out for itself, trying to get the utmost benefits whether in riches or health.

I am glad that this was buried with the past and that in my time there was order and fun on Christmas morning and a certain dignity that was not characteristic of Sundays during the year. Although Christmas Day could fall on any day of the week, it always felt like Sunday and it was, in itself, more important than any Sunday.

Christmas Day was one of rest and relaxation. There was not much company or many guests and dinner was not as special as on Christmas Eve. There might be liver or pork or even fish again, except in certain sections of Sweden where goose was served on Christmas Day. But here again, people had their own traditions concerning foods, and each province followed its own customs. It was always festive though, and whatever the food, it was served in the best room of the house.

But it was a quiet day and a long one. The day after Christmas was also a holiday called *Annandagen*, which means the day following a big holiday. In Sweden, it was also Saint Stephen's Day, a gay day when parties were given and when the children were free to roam and run about, a day filled with cheer. There was no church service; nothing special took place; people just took life easy, visited friends and neighbors, and were cheery and gay because the Christmas season was in full swing.

EIGHT

IN THE Swedish home, the next most important event of the holiday season, following Christmas Eve, was the robbing or plundering of the Christmas tree. This was a delightful custom; and although it is not as old a tradition as some of the others, it has become a permanent one which will remain for many years in the future. In my youth this Christmas festivity promised the most fun for us children, and we looked forward to a day completely free from the restraint of rules. It was a day of freedom, filled with joy and happiness for old and young alike.

The Christmas tree in Sweden had a special mission. It provided for each household the gayest celebration of the year. There was nothing serious at this celebration as there was on Christmas Eve. It was a time when family friends were invited to a party, which might take place anytime between Christmas Day and January thirteenth, and the invitations were usually given by word of mouth on Christmas Day following the *Jul-otta*. But after the thirteenth of January, twenty days after Christmas, there could be no Chrismas-tree robbings. As every day of the year has a name according to the Swedish almanac, this day, January 13, was called *Knut* day; and "after twenty days, on *Knut*, we dance the Christmas tree out." In Swedish it rhymes in this manner:

På tjugondag Knut
Dansar jul-granen ut.

What fun it was on Christmas Day, at that early morning hour, waiting for the invitations.

After wishing one another a very Merry Christmas, the ladies would sweetly say, "Would your family give our family the pleasure of your company at our tree plundering on January second?"

And the affirmative answer came cheerfully back, followed by a similar question.

"We would love to come. And will you join us for ours two days later on January fourth?"

Everybody had to get their date set because almost every house in which there were children wanted to have a tree-plundering party. It seems to me, as I remember now, that the whole Christmas season was just one big gay, happy party.

Again the house was made ready for feasting. The spruce mat outside the front door and the one at the kitchen door were sure to get new branches. These were taken directly from the forest, broken into the right lengths and crisscrossed over each other to make a firm fir rug for snowy feet to be wiped on. I always thought that the spruce mat made the house look cheery. And the smell from it, that pure newly cut spruce smell, permeated the house when the door was opened to the great out of doors. The spruce boughs were such a beautiful shade of green too, that they made a striking contrast against the red painted house.

For this occasion, the Christmas tree was always in the center of the best room. Fresh white candles had replaced the half-burned ones, but other than that the decorations remained as before. A long table was usually placed against the wall; and on it, according to the number of children attending the party, were paper bags and red apples, one for each child, with plenty of space between the bags for the goodies that would be piled there later.

Another table was set for the adults. This was the fanciest of all coffee tables, spread with plenty of sandwiches, all the special coffee bread, and the many varieties of cookies and cakes. And there was always a big *torte* heaped with whipped cream, making it resemble a small snow mountain. The best silver and crystal plates were used and to top off the magnificent refreshments, there was a large crystal bowl filled with sliced oranges covered with powdered sugar.

Cups, spoons, and everything else were set out early so that all the hostess had to do while the guests were there was to make the coffee and see to it that everything was properly served. The silver coffee service, still sparkling from the Christmas cleaning, was put to good use now. The biggest copper coffeepot stood on the shiny black wood stove in the kitchen to assure enough coffee even if everyone drank two or three cups. When the guests arrived, the whole family was on hand to greet them and make them feel at home.

Since most families in those days had quite a few children, the house filled up quickly; and when all the guests had arrived, the dancing around the Christmas tree began. Everyone took part, from the youngest to the oldest. After the live candles had been lit, everyone joined hands and began to walk around and around the Christmas tree. If there was a baby in the group, he was held in someone's arms.

As they walked around the tree, they sang songs that had been passed down from generation to generation. Perhaps this one was the most popular Christmas-tree song.

> Nu är det Jul igen,
> Nu är det Jul igen.
> Och Julen varar intil Paska.
> Men de va inte sant,
> Men de va inte sant,
> För där emellan kommer fastan.

The song says that Christmas has come again and will last until Easter, although between the two comes Lent.

The singing and dancing went on . . .

> Anders Persons stuga
> Står i ljusan låga.
> All ljusen brinna oppsan!
> Hej hoppsan i galoppsan!
> Inte gifter jag mig bråttsam!

Most of the songs were without any real meaning, just silly songs making much out of almost nothing, rhyming about marriages and burning houses and so on, simply for fun. But everyone sang with lusty voices while they danced round and round the tree. After a while, the older people sat down to rest for a few moments, some gasping for breath, others impatient to get started again.

Singing games with gestures were next on the agenda.

> The fox runs over the ice now,
> The fox runs over the ice now,
> May I please,
> May I please,
> Sing the song of the baker.

At the end of the first verse, everyone knelt down, bent forward, and clapped his hands on the bare floor many times, making a loud noise and singing as he clapped:

> This is the way the baker does.
> Wherever he stands, wherever he goes,
> May I please,
> May I please,
> Sing the song of the butcher.

The song had at least ten verses and the singers mimicked old men, old women, boys, girls, shoemakers, tailors, chimney cleaners, and the parson. There was a certain appropriate motion for each character and the song was accompanied by shouts of laughter.

After a while parlor games were played. There were riddles, guessing games, and winking games. The old were again young, and the children almost forgot that they were playing with grownups who did not usually indulge in children's games.

And so the afternoon drifted into evening as the clock ticked away the minutes, and suddenly the aroma of freshly brewed coffee filled the house, and it was time for the youngsters to rob the tree.

As the adults watched, the children, on a given signal, began to prance about the tree, picking it clean of all its splendor, placing their trophies in a big heap on the long table where the bags were. Down came the gingerbread men and the Christmas bucks, the confect candy and the colorful tassel candy, the *tomtes* and the angels. When all the goodies had been cleaned off, an adult would remove the candles and apples. The ladies arranged the goodies in piles, dividing them so that each child had an equal share. Cookies and cake were added to each pile, and finally a drink called *saft*, a punch made of fruit juice, was served to the children, who on this day were the honored guests.

The Christmas tree stood there alone in its green nakedness, stripped of all its glory, until the people moved toward it, grabbing hold of its branches. If the gay celebrators could not get hold of a branch, they held on to each other as they danced out with the tree: around the room, down the long hall, through the large kitchen and the back hall, singing and shouting, and finally out into the yard, where the tree was left in a lonely corner to be chopped up for firewood or just to be forgotten and blown about by the strong north wind in the dark winter night.

So the tree's beautiful story ended. Another year, another tree would be the center of the Christmas festivities, only to be plundered and cast away.

But inside the well-lighted house the gaiety continued. The children were delighted with their tidbits, and what they could not eat was placed in the paper bags to be saved for the next day. One thing that was never stored in the bags was the quarter of an orange given to each child. This was the most treasured of all the goodies. During my childhood, oranges came to Sweden only at Christmas time, at least for the common people. Never had anything tasted so good, nor was anything as exciting as biting into that juicy fruit; the memory will never be forgotten by some of us, for that rare treat was the highlight of a wonderful plundering party.

The adults enjoyed their coffee and raved about the treats which the table contained, giving special recognition to their hostess for her masterful baking. Compliments came easily from the lips of the happy, contented people.

As the Christmas season drew to a close, only one more celebration remained, that of Epiphany, the day of the Three Kings, on January sixth. What could be lovelier than to rejoice with the star-boys whose tradition dates back to the seventeenth century? It originated in Germany where the first boys were led by their schoolmaster through a large city, singing and carrying a shiny star in front of them, symbolizing the star of Bethlehem. Somehow this lovely custom found its way through Denmark, across the small patch of water that separates Denmark and Sweden, and found a home among the Swedish people, who love to take a new and unusual custom and elaborate on it until it becomes their own.

The star-boys marched, singing, through cities and towns, dressed in long white robes and carrying the shining star and burning candles. On their heads they wore ornate cone-shaped hats which made them feel very important.

Christmas would not be complete without our seeing the star-boys and listening to their singing and perhaps reaching out a hand to give them a gift.

As the story of Christmas in my memory begins with the beautiful Saint Lucia who came to us from Sicily, so it ends with the star-boys who came to us from Germany, both colorful traditions that have brought a sense of friendship and understanding to Sweden, a country overflowing with folklore and hearsay and superstition—some of it foolish perhaps; some, wise; some evil, but more, good.

Truth and fiction are mixed together in a shiny big red Christmas bowl, but underneath it all, I feel, we can trace the reality and warmth that have been in the heart of a frozen winterland throughout the many hundreds of years it has existed.

The Christmas season, no matter how beautiful it is, always ends. The lights are put out, the tree discarded, and people return to their normal living. But in the minds of the children, who are the saddest to see it end, are always the thoughts that in only a little more than eleven months, one dark cold early December morning they will awake again to the aroma of baking cookies drifting through the house. And their hearts beat a little faster as they count on their fingers . . . today is the day before the day before the day . . . and so on and on until they can say "the day before the dipping-day." Then Christmas all over again.

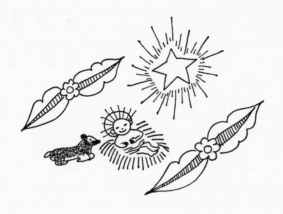

NINE

So I come to the end of my "Once Upon a Christmas Time." It has been fascinating to wander back into childhood days and even further into the years when the celebrations began. But time is marching on and each generation is building its own world, a world that will someday, in turn, become a heritage or a tradition or just a memory recorded in a history book for those who will dwell in the world of tomorrow. I have written this with my heart instead of my mind, for the recollections are all tender and meaningful.

As I look out at Christmases in this new age with its neon signs and artificial glitter, its loud music, its rushing and pushing and buying of gifts, its eating out in fancy restaurants, and its different kinds of parties, given the world over, my heart cries a little and there is a dull ache somewhere within me. I would like to call out to the world to be still . . . to stop just long enough to think and remember . . . to retrieve all those precious things we lost way back there in time—somewhere—when Christmas was home, when it was family, when it was heartfelt, and when all the beauty that could be contained in a few holidays was reserved for just the family and friends to share.

It was not elaborate or fancy, but it was good and warm and real. We let the clock stand still and took time to be ourselves, to let the very best in us come to the surface. That was our Christmas gift to each other, given in love.

That love reflects the love of the first Christmas morning in Bethlehem when the star grew dim and a mother and father bowed tenderly over a tiny babe. We still sing "O Little Town of Bethlehem" and especially here in America our Christmas carols are a beautiful tradition. People who remember have told me how, long ago, singing together as families around the piano, those carols brought Christmas right into their midst. They were all there, the old, the young, and even the very tiny, and the music filled their home with the voices of happy people. I am so glad that we have those carols and that they are played every Christmas season to bring a message to those whose ears and hearts are open to listening.

In many homes the first Sunday of December still means the beginning of Advent, when the family will light that first tall candle. This is not just a regional event; it is celebrated in homes and churches in Sweden and Germany and in countries all over the world. It proclaims the glad tidings of the great light promised to a weary world. Each Sunday a new candle is lit until, on the Sunday before Christmas, the fourth and last candle is set aflame. There is still hope for our world as long as families light these candles, as long as they sing the carols, read the Christmas story together, and rejoice over the gift given to the world—that light so bright that no darkness can hide it. It is this faith in our age and this hope that makes our modern Christmas real and alive.

There is much beauty in the world today and much goodness and kindness and generosity. People open their hearts and pocketbooks to share with those in need. At no other time of the year are the poor and the sick and the bereaved remembered more generously than at Christmas time. And every time we share, we praise God who gave that first Christmas gift to the whole world!

For God so loved the world, that He gave His only begotten Son, That whosoever that believeth in Him should not perish, but have everlasting life.

That gift is as real today as on the morning it was given. It is free for every person to accept as his own. It is a tremendous gift, so immense in its greatness that hundreds of years have not diminished its grandeur, and time will never destroy it.

In every heart that receives God's gift the star still shines! The angels still sing! The shepherds still journey to the stable! And the wisemen still come from afar. And because of this, new lights appear in darkness, new hope is given to captives. And as long as there is a Christmas, no matter what people of ill will try to do, they will not be able to put out the light that was lit two thousand years ago and that outshines all other lights in the world.

Christmas is ours—all of us together—no matter what country we come from, when we accept God's gift of the Little Child, who was, Himself, the light of the very first once-upon-a-Christmas-time.